SAVING

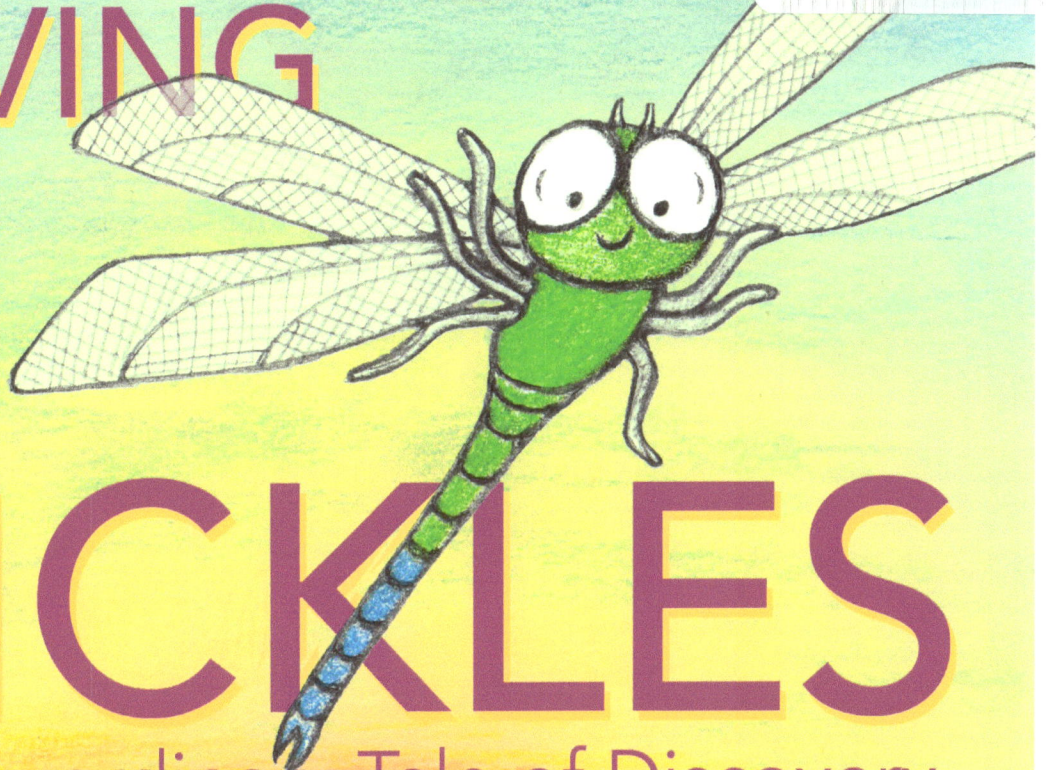

PICKLES

an Extraordinary Tale of Discovery

by Marilynn Barr

LAB202302EP

LITTLE
ACORN
BOOKS

Includes
Hands-On
Projects

SAVING PICKLES
an Extraordinary Tale of Discovery

featuring

Little Projects for Little Hands

by Marilynn Barr

- Two hands-on projects are included in the back of this book.

- Each project is designed with directions and patterns to actually cut out.

- Each project features a *Give a Helping Hand* logo ✋ Give a helping hand. alert for adult helpers.

- Beginning and advanced learners may require some assistance completing either project.

- Scissor icons ✂ identify the patterns to cut out.

LAB202302EP
ISBN
978-1-946557-10-0

Published by
Little Acorn Books™
Greensboro, NC

an imprint of
Little Acorn Associates, Inc.
Promoting Early Skills for a Lifetime™
https://www.littleacornbooks.com

Dedicated to bug fans of all ages

~

Thank you to the British Dragonfly Society and the Dragonfly Society of the Americas for permission to include information from their respective websites to share with you.

When I was young, I was a bug fan. I played with creepy crawlies at the playground in Riverside Park but dragonflies always made me nervous and I don't know when bugs became icky, but…

During a particular family vacation, I discovered fascinating facts about dragonflies and damselflies. And to be perfectly honest, I am excited to share what I learned. Did you know dragonflies and damselflies have up to 30,000 eye lenses? It's extraordinary!

~

Marilynn Barr was born and raised in New York City.
Today, she lives and works in North Carolina.
She loves to paint, draw, work with clay, sew, learn new things and about old things,
And she creates books for young children—always
promoting early skills for a lifetime™.

For more information about
Dragonflies & Damselflies
Visit

British Dragonfly Society
https://british-dragonflies.org.uk

and the

Dragonfly Society of the Americas
https://www.dragonflysocietyamericas.org

It was nine or ten years ago,
during a family vacation, when a black cloud
led to an extraordinary tale of discovery.

Two cars packed tighter than a box of crayons
with three adults and four children, many suitcases
and boxes full of food; blankets and pillows; stuffed
animals, water toys, beach chairs, and more, arrived
at the beach on the coast of North Carolina.

It didn't matter what we brought with us
because the ultimate goal was fun
in the sand and the salty water.

On the second day, sometime after dinner,
I watched as Sarah stopped her bike
and shouted, "Look!"

At just about the same moment,
Sky asked, "What is that?"

"I believe that's a dragonfly," I answered.

Sarah scrambled onto the deck, pointing and continuing to shout. "Look, look, look!"

Avery ran to the window to see
a few dragonflies whiz by.

A black cloud was moving towards us
from the north and the sky directly above us
grew dark enough for the deck lights to turn on.

Ashton shouted,

"It's a mob!"

as she ran up the deck stairs.

Hundreds, maybe thousands, of dragonflies whizzed past us.

The mob maneuvered to the left, to the right, and over our heads.

But not one dragonfly crashed into any of us not even into Skyler, who was flailing her arms to keep them away.

As fast as it approached,

the black cloud,

the mob, was gone.

"Oh no," Ashton cried out.

"There's one trapped inside the deck light."

Yes there was a single dragonfly trapped inside the deck light.

Maybe it made a wrong turn.
Maybe it got turned around in the mob.
The mob was moving so fast.
Maybe it was one of the younger dragonflies that didn't have much experience flying with the mob.

Either way, it couldn't find its way out.
And the bulb had to be getting hot.

Well, I am not a bug fan.
Ashton wasn't either.

Julie, the girl's mom, heard us squawking.

Who would free the dragonfly before it was too late.
"You do it!" "No, you do it!"

"What is going on?" She asked.

We both stopped.
Without another word,
we both pointed toward the deck light.

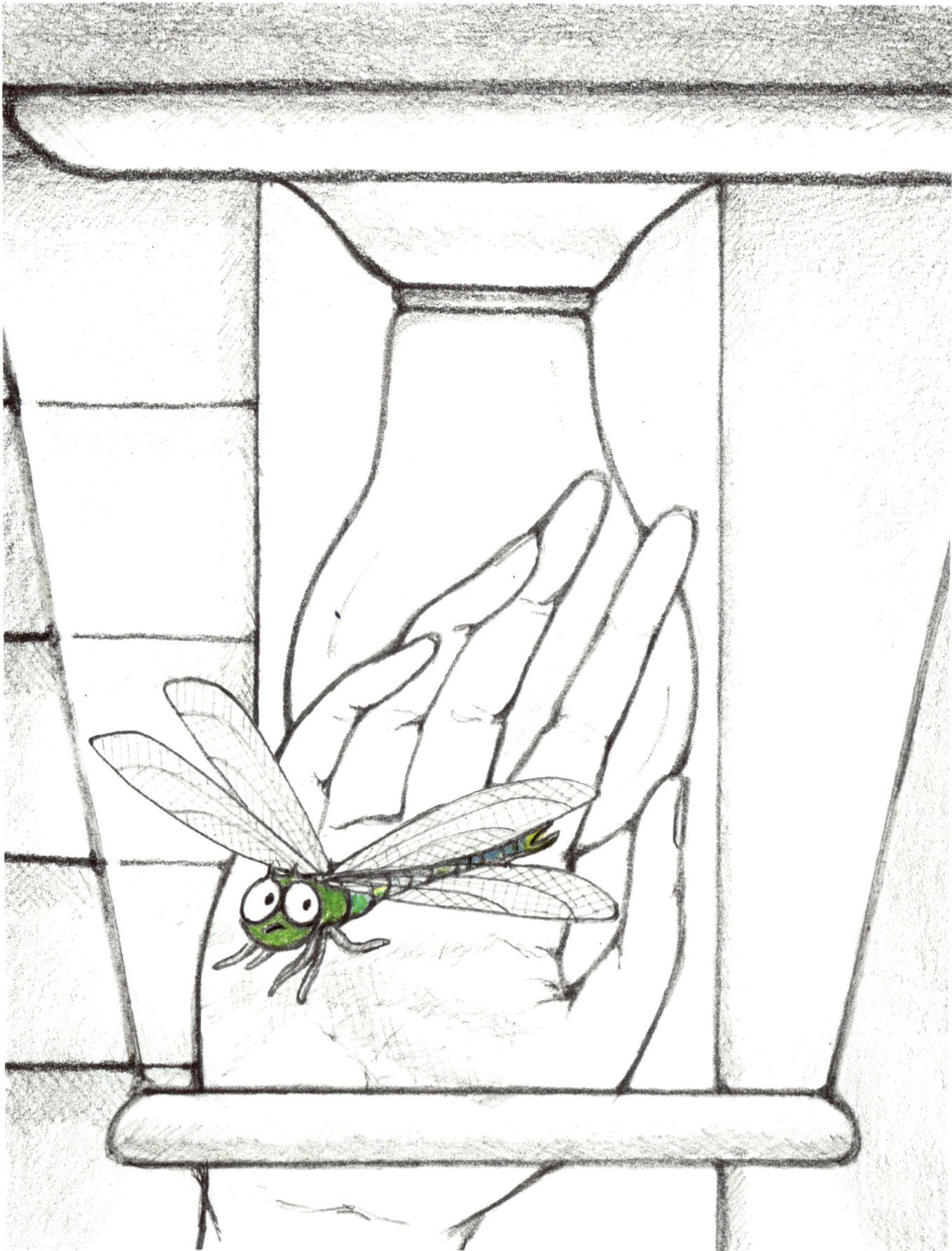

Julie laughed.

She walked over to the deck light.

She reached inside and

scooped the dragonfly to freedom.

The girls cheered as the dragonfly
flew across the deck.

I said, "We should give that little guy a name."
Skyler immediately shouted,
"Let's call it Pickles!"

And so, Pickles hovered for just a moment,
then turned and flew south,
in the same direction as the mob.

The girls asked,

"Do you think Pickles will find the others?"

"Where did they come from?"

"Where are they going?"

We will never know the answers to those questions but for the rest of our vacation days and after we returned home, I searched for and discovered extraordinary facts about *Odonata*.

ODONATA FACTS
About Damselflies & Dragonflies

Did You Know?

- ☐ *Odonata* is an order or super-family of flying insects.

- ☐ There are two suborders or smaller families of *Odonata*: dragonflies and damselflies.

- ☐ Dragonflies are larger and stouter members of the *Anisoptera* suborder, which means "different wings."

- ☐ Damselflies are skinny and members of the *Zygoptera* suborder, which means "same wings."

- ☐ Dragonflies and damselflies do not have a *pupal* stage like other insect groups.

- ☐ New adults are called *tenerals*.

- ☐ Dragonflies do not bite or sting and they do not attack people.

- ☐ They both live underwater in ponds, rivers, and streams as *nymphs*, also called *larvae*, or *naiads*.

- ☐ They both are *carnivores* and use their bottom jaws to catch prey.

ODONATA FACTS
About Damselflies & Dragonflies

☐ Dragonflies and damselflies have compound eyes with up to 30,000 lenses and they both have excellent eyesight.

☐ A dragonfly's eyes are very large and usually wrap around and touch at the top of its round head.

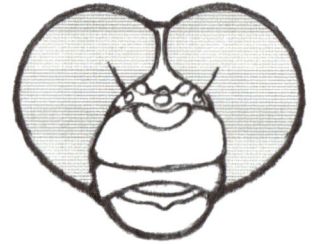

☐ A damselfly's eyes are also very large but never touch.

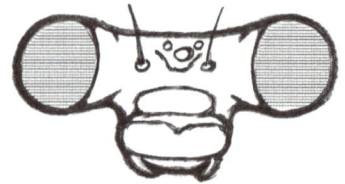

☐ Dragonflies and damselflies have two (2) very short antennae.

☐ The long section that looks like a tail is actually the *abdomen*. It is flexible and has 10 segments. This is the food processing and reproductive center of both dragonflies and damselflies.

☐ One might call a dragonfly's *thorax* a power station because it supports its head, legs, and wings.

DRAGONFLY FACTS

Anisoptera = Different Wings

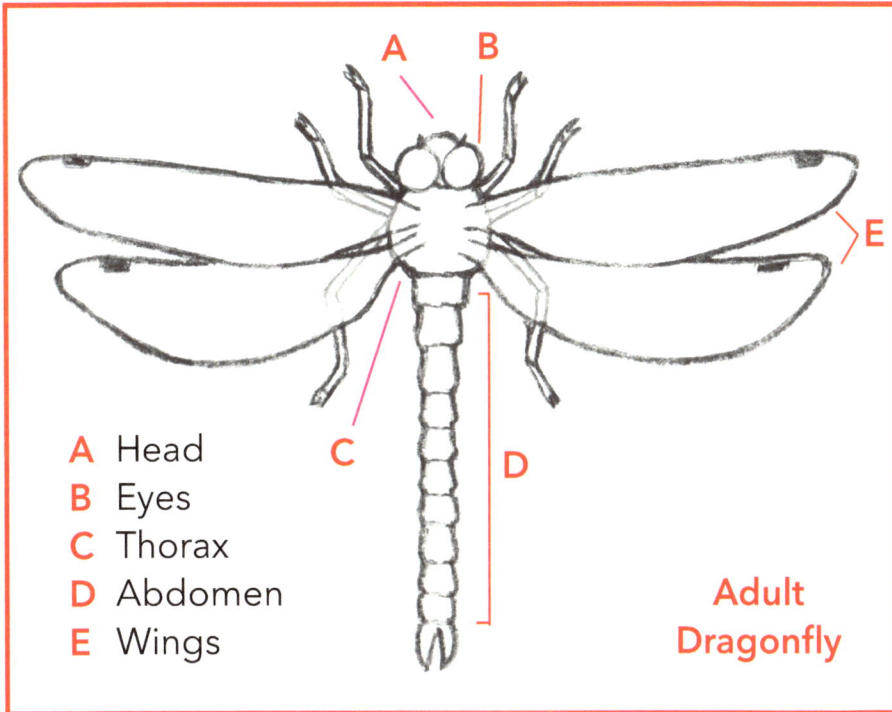

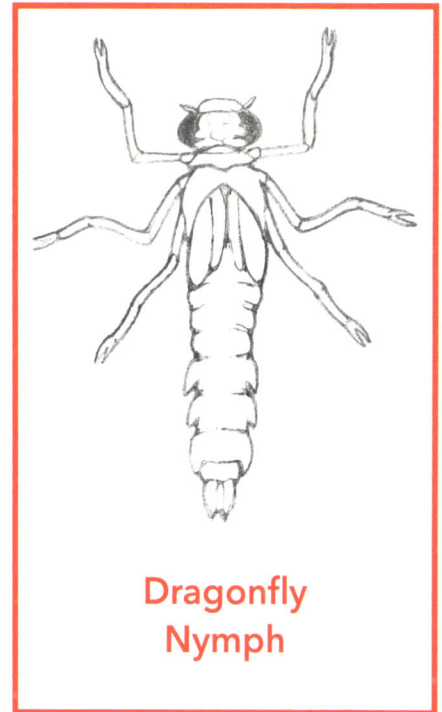

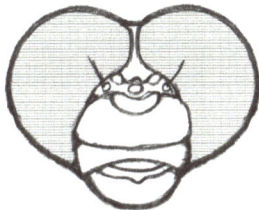

A Head
B Eyes
C Thorax
D Abdomen
E Wings

Adult Dragonfly

Dragonfly Nymph

Eyes
A dragonfly's eyes are very large and usually wrap around and touch at the top of its round head.

Antennae
Dragonflies have two very short antennae.

Structure
Like all insects, dragonflies have six legs. A dragonfly's body is made up of three (3) segments, the *head*, *thorax*, and an *abdomen* that has ten (10) segments.

Wings
A dragonfly's wings are transparent. Their hind wings are shorter and broader than its front wings. When it is at rest its wings are outstretched.

Larvae, Nymph, or Naiad
Dragonfly *nymphs* live most of their lives underwater.

Adults
New adults are called *tenerals* and they change colors as they grow older.

DAMSELFLY FACTS

Zygoptera = Same Wings

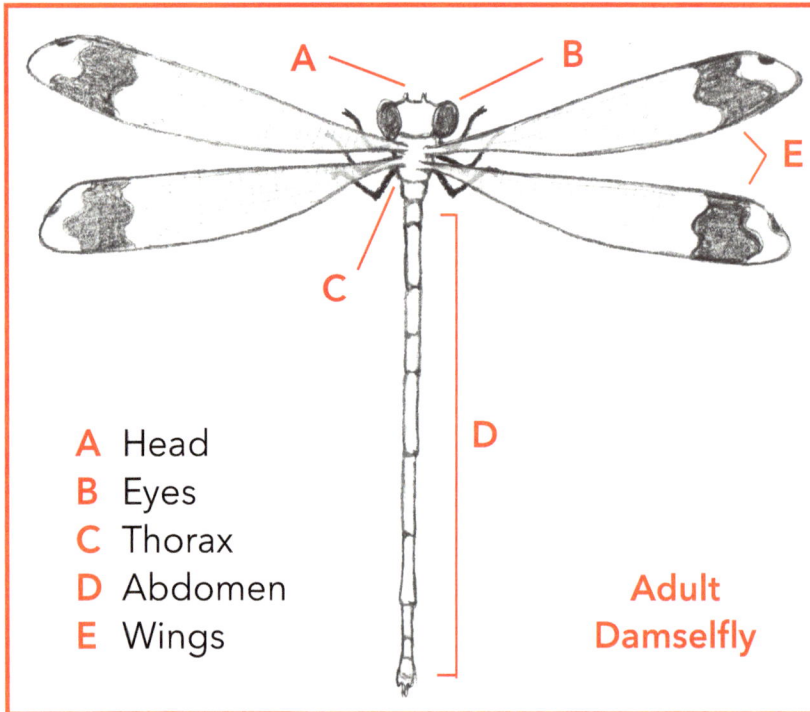

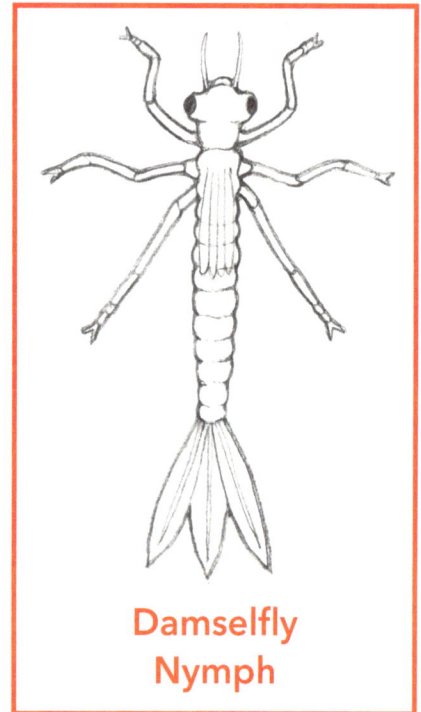

A **Head**
B **Eyes**
C **Thorax**
D **Abdomen**
E **Wings**

Adult Damselfly

Damselfly Nymph

Eyes
A damselfly's eyes are very large but never touch.

Antennae
Damselflies have two very short antennae.

Structure
A damselfly's body is made up of three (3) segments, the *head*, *thorax*, and an *abdomen* that has ten (10) segments. Like all insects, damselflies have six legs.

Wings
Damselfly wings are transparent and equal in size and shape. When a damselfly is at rest, its wings are folded together, above or over its abdomen.

Larvae, Nymph, or Naiad
Damselfly *nymphs* live most of their lives underwater.

Adults
New adults are called *tenerals* and they change colors as they grow older.

ODONATA FACTS

About Damselflies & Dragonflies

☐ The largest prehistoric dragonfly was the *Permian Meganeuropsis Permiana*. It had a wingspan of 27 to 29 inches or 70 to 75 centimeters. That is almost as wide as a 21st century skateboard deck.

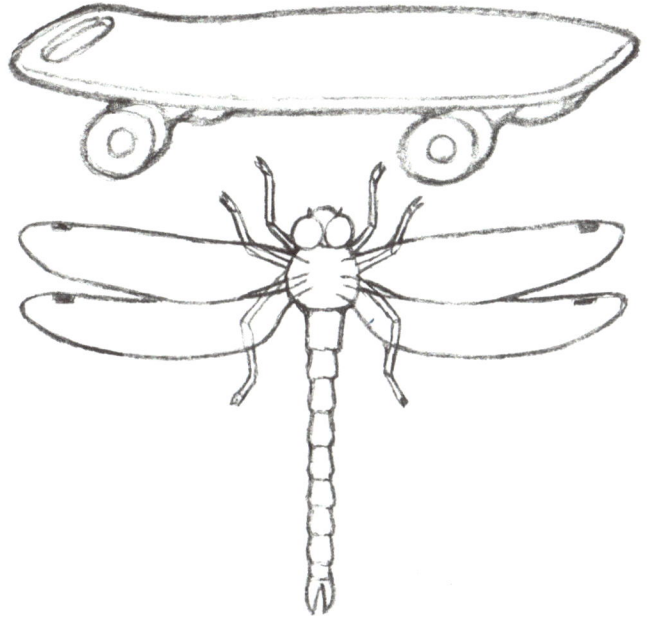

☐ Today, the largest damselfly is the *Megaloprepus Coeralatus*. It is found in Central America. It has a wingspan over 7 inches or 19 centimeters. That is wider than a United States dollar bill.

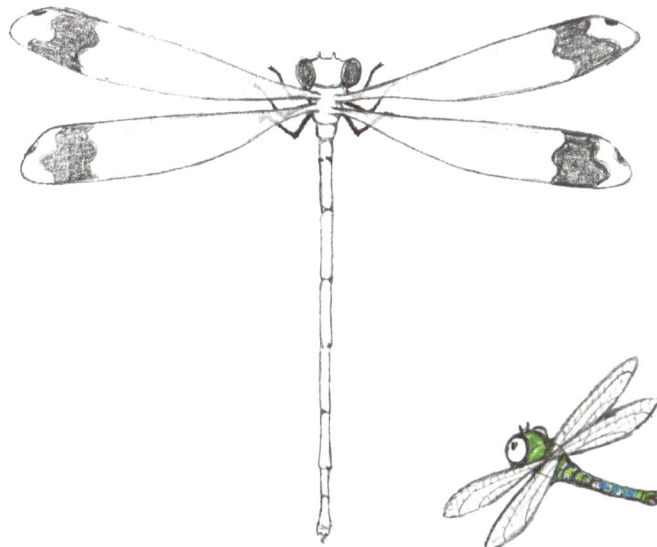

ODONATA FACTS
About Damselflies & Dragonflies

☐ The *Scarlet Dwarf* is the smallest dragonfly found in East Asia. Its wingspan is a little over 3/4 of an inch, or 20 millimeters. That is almost the size of a United States nickel.

☐ Dragonflies can fly up to 35 miles per hour or 54 kilometers.

☐ Some dragonflies can travel up to 11,000 miles or 18,000 kilometers, in one flight. Imagine that! A dragonfly could travel from North Carolina in the United States to Christmas Island, a distance of 10,164 miles or 16,358 kilometers.

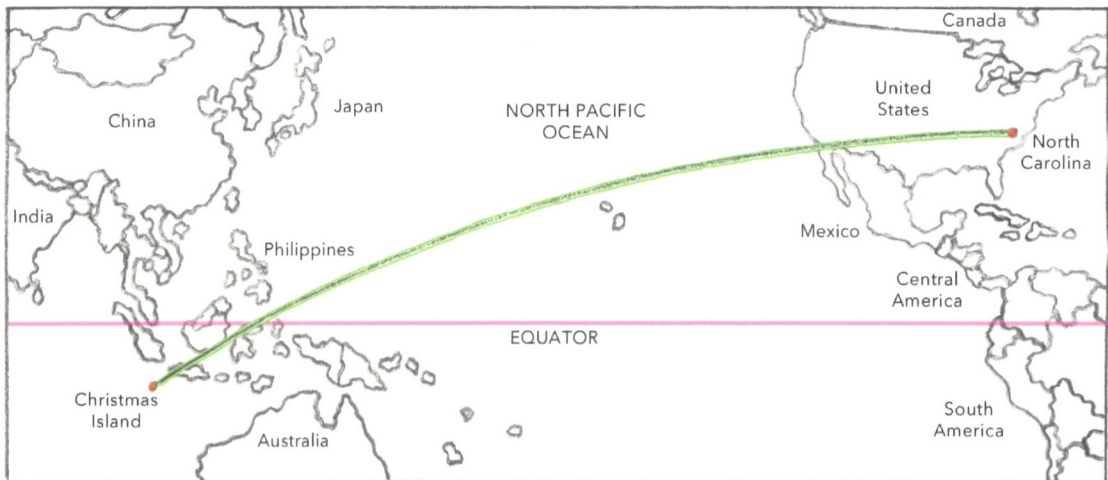

☐ And dragonflies migrate. There is little research to explain why, but many continue to investigate.

IT'S A DAMSELFLY PROJECT

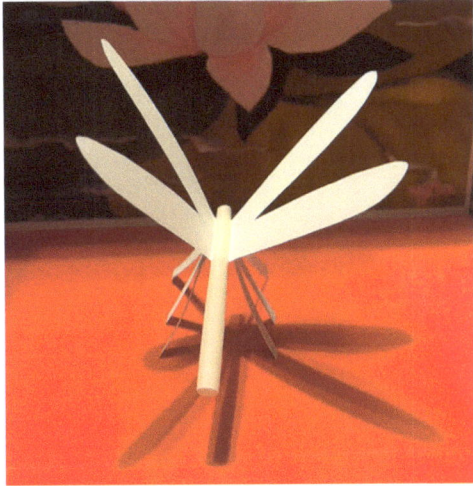

What You Will Need:

Damselfly Patterns (p. 47)
one (1) straw
scissors
ruler
pencil
stapler

2.

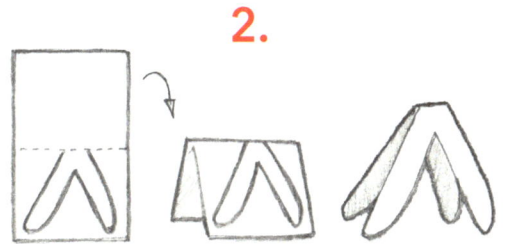

Fold and cut out.

What to Do:

1. Cut out the Damselfly Patterns.
2. Fold each pattern in half as shown here and cut out.
3. Cut a straw in half.
4. Use a pencil to crease each side of one end of the straw as shown here.
5. Cut a slit along each crease.
6. Staple the wing and leg patterns together along the fold line.
7. Slide the wings and legs into the slit.

4.

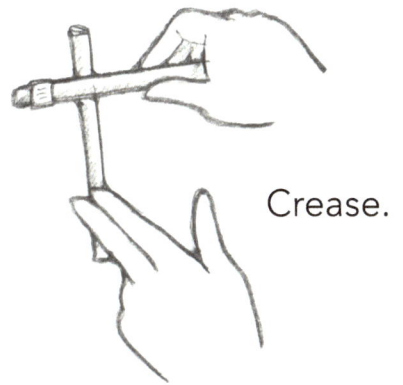

Crease.

5.

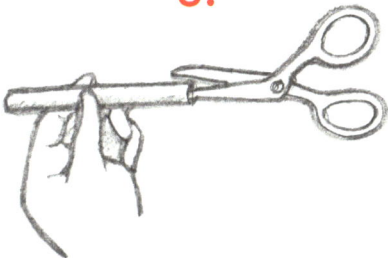

Slit.

6.

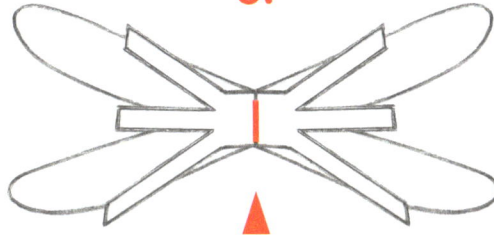

Staple.

7.

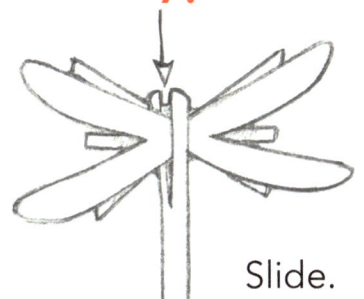

Slide.

IT'S A DAMSELFLY PROJECT

Give a helping hand.

What to Do: (continued)

8. Fold over each set of wings as shown below.
9. Fold over each set of legs as shown below.
10. Adjust the wings and legs then display your damselfly.

Note: The wings can lay flat, as if in-flight, or folded up, as if at rest.

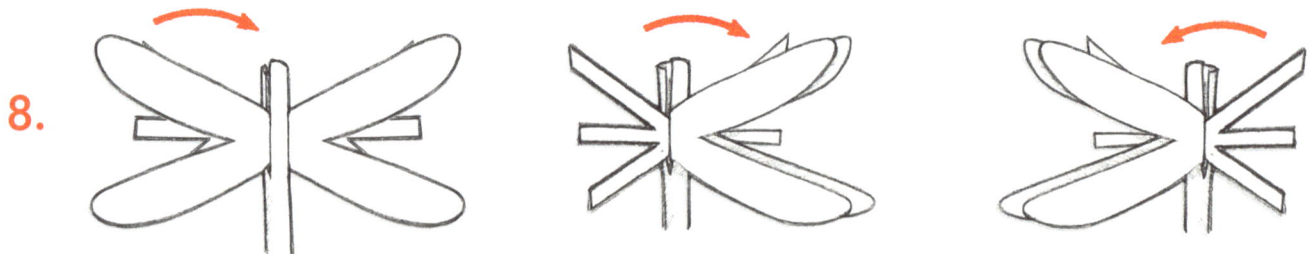

8. Fold over each set of wings.

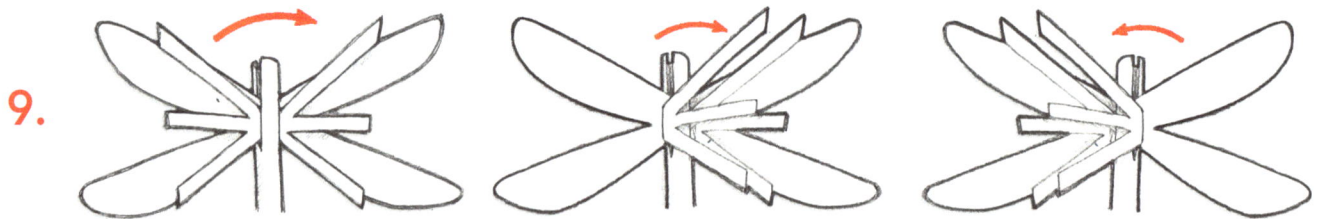

9. Fold over each set of legs.

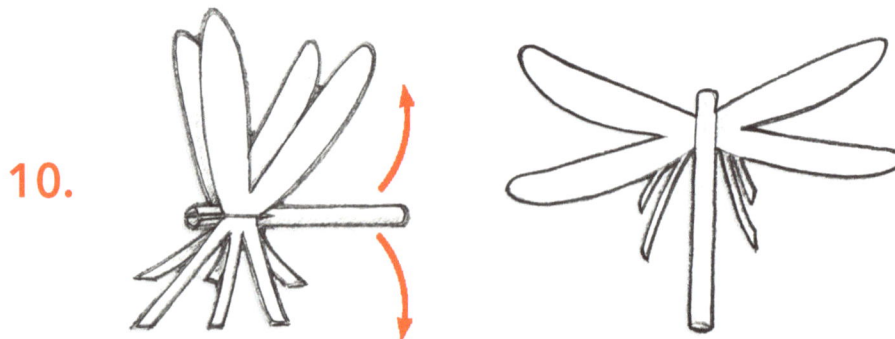

10. Adjust the wings and legs to display.

DAMSELFLY PATTERNS

Give a helping hand.

WINGS

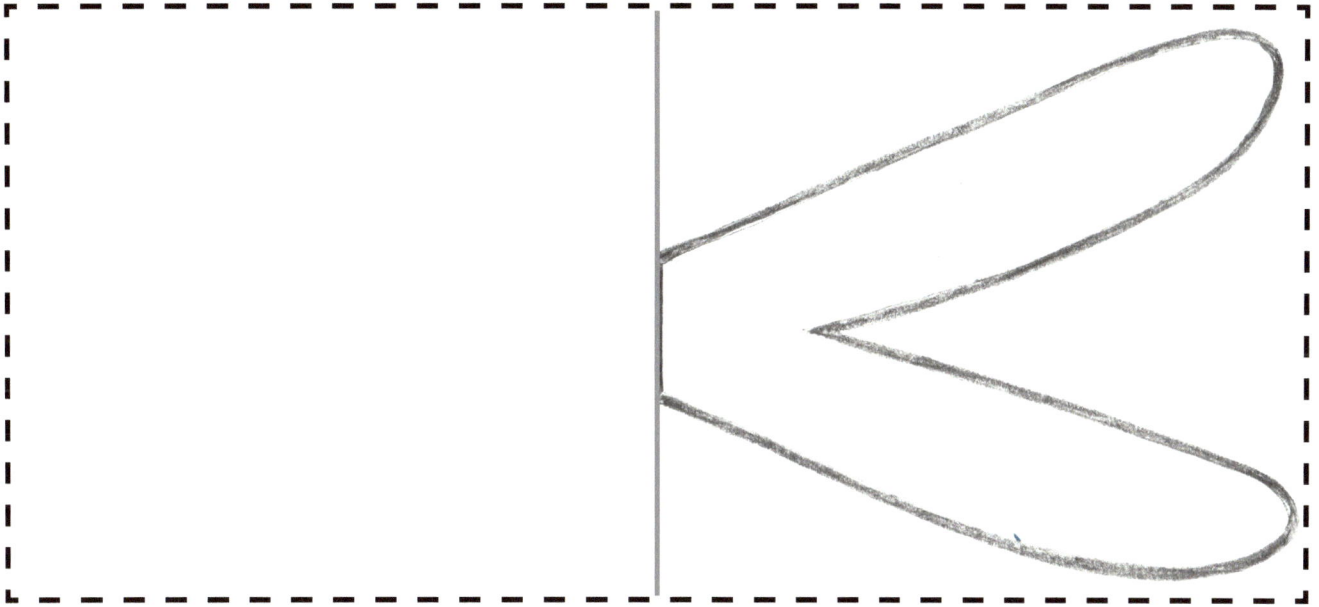

Cut out this pattern along the dotted line.

Fold and cut out the wings as shown here.

LEGS

Cut out this pattern along the dotted line.

Fold and cut out the legs as shown here.

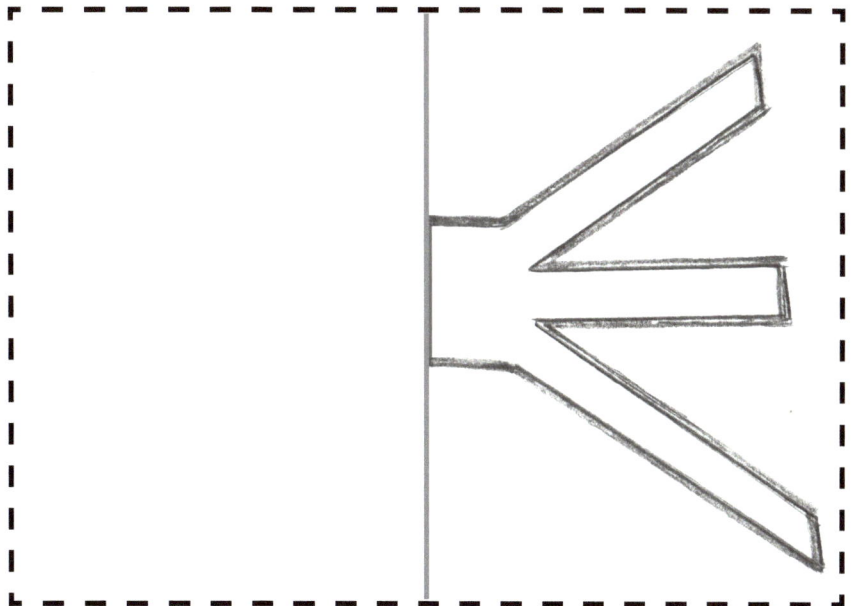

This page is intentionally blank.

PICKLES THE DRAGONFLY PROJECT

What You Will Need:

Pickles Dragonfly Pattern (p. 51)
crayons
paint & paintbrush (optional)
scissors
glue
clothespin
paper towel tube

Note:
There are two
(2) patterns on
page 51.
Share one with
a friend.

What to Do:

1. Color and cut out a Pickles Dragonfly Pattern.
2. Use crayons or paint to color a paper towel tube.
3. Apply glue to one flat side of a clothespin.
4. Attach the clothespin, glue side down, to the back of your dragonfly.
5. Pinch the clothespin to attach your dragonfly to the paper towel tube.

Option:

Decorate a curtain or a lamp shade with your dragonfly.

3. and 4.

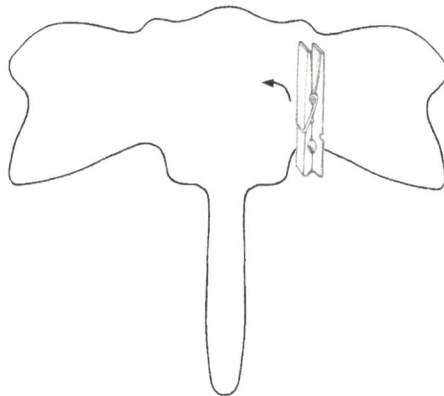

Apply glue and attach.

5.

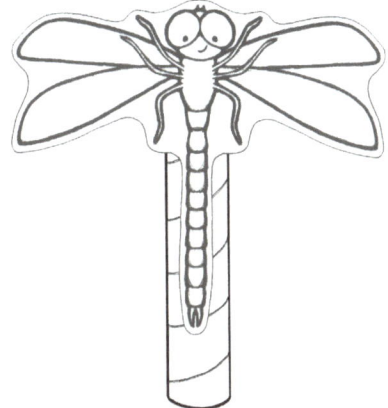

Pinch and attach.

This page is intentionally blank.

PICKLES DRAGONFLY PATTERNS

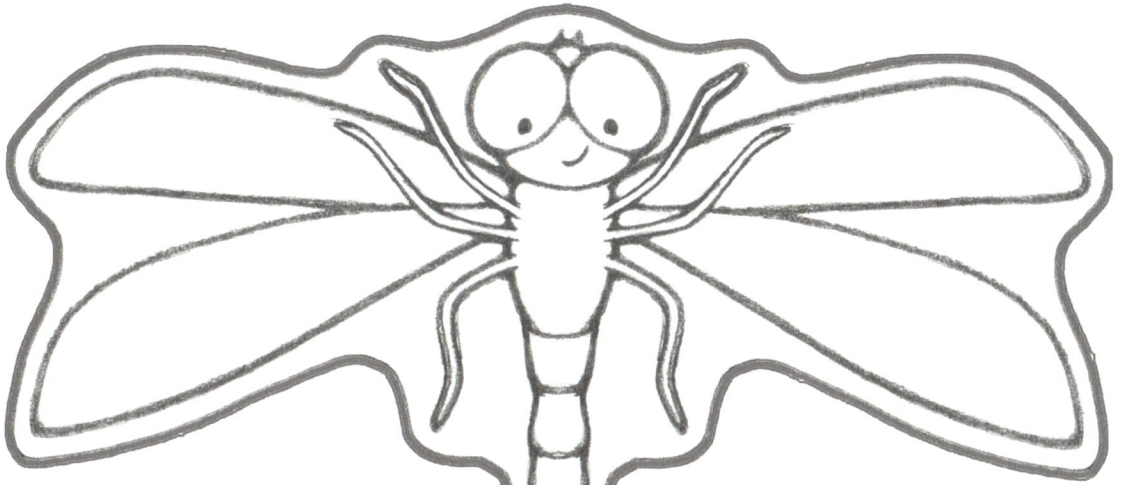

Cut out along the
bold outline.

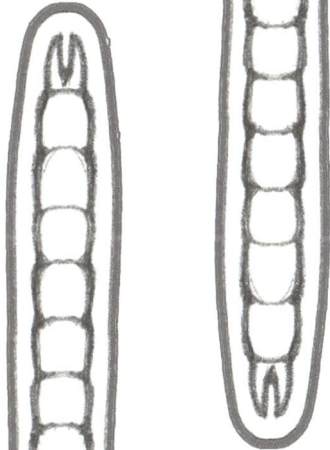

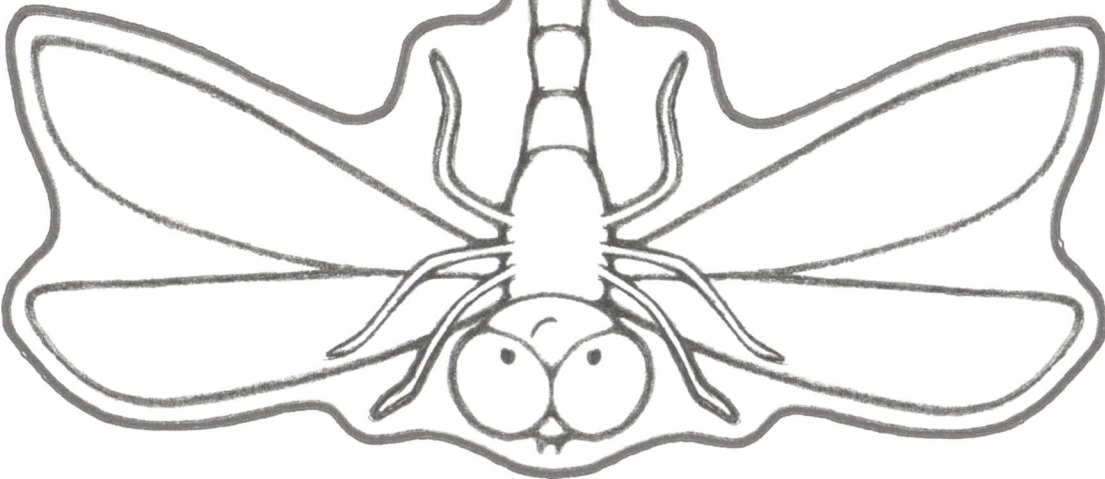

Cut out along the
bold outline.

SAVING PICKLES

an Extraordinary Tale of Discovery

by Marilynn Barr

- Do you know how large a prehistoric dragonfly was?
- Do you know where the largest damselfly is today?
- Do you know where to find the smallest dragonfly?
- Do you know how far a dragonfly can travel?
- Do you know dragonflies migrate?

It's extraordinary!

Look inside to learn more.

LAB202302EP

LITTLE
ACORN
BOOKS

Includes
Hands-On
Projects

9 781946 557100